WISDOM OF
KUAN YIN

An Oracle Book of Guidance & Prayers
from the Divine Feminine

Alana Fairchild

BLUE ANGEL®
PUBLISHING

Wisdom of Kuan Yin

Published by Blue Angel Publishing
80 Glen Tower Drive, Glen Waverley,
Victoria, Australia 3150
E-mail: info@blueangelonline.com
Website: www.blueangelonline.com

Artwork by Zeng Hao
Edited by Tanya Graham

Blue Angel is a registered trademark of Blue Angel Gallery Pty. Ltd.

ISBN: 978-1-922161-31-4

Om Kuan Chi Yin Poosa!
Om Mani Padme Hum!

Introduction

Kuan Yin is the Mother of Compassion. She guides us into our enlightenment, which is being able to live in harmony and unity with the Love that is, and surrendering into that Love. Enlightenment is not meant to be a distant spiritual goal, but something that we can choose to live at any time, by choosing love, kindness, compassion and wisdom over fear, judgement, anger or separation from the Source, the Divine Feminine, that seeks to nourish us so that we blossom into the fullness of our being.

No matter what your religious, cultural or spiritual background, Kuan Yin loves you without condition. Her compassion is legendary and with good reason – there is nothing that you could do to evoke judgement from her, even in your darkest or most fearful moments, her gentle heart-light shines forgiveness and peace upon you and your life path. Even so, she is not indulgent! She will call to you to believe in yourself, to find your inner strength and to allow for your own healing by taking responsibility for the choices you make in your life.

She is the gentle mother, but she is fierce in her love for your soul and she will guide you to your best life – even if sometimes that feels challenging. She does this because she loves you and she knows that you are capable of so much more than you realise. Sometimes we just need the divine encouragement to come back to our hearts, to let go of fear, anxiety and despair, and realise that even if we don't quite know how, life will sort itself out, and our path is blessed whenever we simply ask for her help. We do this by taking a moment and simply saying quietly in our minds or aloud, "Kuan Yin who loves me without condition, please help me now." You can never ask for too much help. She will always assist you and wants you to call for her divine intervention, healing and protection every day if you will.

You are such a beautiful Soul and you have the power to co-create a beautiful life through which your Soul light can radiate and uplift others, reminding them of the way of love rather than fear. You can be a source of great light, healing and wisdom on this planet if you so choose. You are drawn to this book because you are ready. You are ready to grow spiritually, to be a guiding light in the evolution of consciousness on this planet, to be brave and to choose love over fear. Come and bask in the loving glow, the guidance and blessings of beloved Kuan Yin as you find her in your own heart and Soul, speaking to you from within. Namaste, Beloved, She sees, honours and nourishes your light now.

Om Kuan Chi Yin Poosa!
Om Mani Padme Hum!

BAMBOO MOON

Did you know that there are no mistakes in the Universe and all events, circumstances, relationships and situations are unfolding in perfection with the timing and intelligence of the divine plan? Any apparent delay is in your favour. If something is happening for you right now, then that is perfect too. Divine timing is perfection. It is safe to trust this now.

*

PRAYER UNDER THE BAMBOO MOON

Kuan Yin, you surrender into the perfection of divine timing, like the bamboo shoots preparing for fast growth and the beautiful moon growing full. Sometimes change is not so obvious and yet growth is happening! Please help me realise all is in accordance with Perfect Timing in my own life and all of my plans, projects and desires now. Fill my heart with your love and peace, beloved Goddess. Let the wisdom of the Bamboo Moon penetrate my Soul. Om Mani Padme Hum.

BLESSINGS OF THE MOON MAIDEN

The Moon Maiden, with her Lucky Hare, brings auspicious tidings of prosperity and abundance to you now. The Universe seeks to replenish, restore and create through you. Allow yourself to receive beyond what you have thought is possible by opening your heart with gratitude now. Let the blessings of good fortune from the beloved Maiden of the Moon, Kuan Yin, flow easily into your life now.

*

A PRAYER TO THE MOON MAIDEN

I now choose to release negative energy, negative beliefs and negative memories connected with abundance, money, relationships, success and wellbeing. I offer these for healing to beloved Moon Maiden, Kuan Yin. May she turn the heaviness of these offerings into golden light. May I receive this golden light into my heart. Good fortune and blessings flow to me now. May I share as I receive. May I flow with joy, abundance and divine grace. Through the blessings of the Divine Kuan Yin, so be it.

BLOSSOMS OF THE SKY DANCER

Kuan Yin dances creative energy and light across the sky, causing blossoms to descend. In the same way, when we tap into our spiritual power of creation, we cause our life and all of life around us, to bloom. Creation is a natural spiritual power within you, beloved. Force can slow down the process. It is time to stop striving and to allow your manifestation to occur. Trust, let go, allow your creation to flow.

*

PRAYER TO THE SKY DANCER

Beloved Kuan Yin, Sky Dancer, blossoming with creation, I am one with the power of the divine feminine. I am one with peace, with creation that will manifest. I am love, I am surrendering, I am Yin, I am blessed. I let go to receive. I let go to flow. Peace in my heart now fertilises my creation to grow. Om Mani Padme Hum.

CALL OF THE DANCING CRANE

Dancing Crane moves through waters and muddy marsh with elegance and grace. The mating call and dance of the Crane is full of beautiful movement and flow. There are times when the astral waters of our emotional life become stagnant and will benefit from the healing movement, grace and beauty of the Dancing Crane. The Call of the Dancing Crane is a reminder that sound can be healing too. This is particularly so when your thoughts, beliefs and emotional patterns do not support you in living the spiritual destiny you were born to live.

*

A PRAYER TO THE CALL OF THE DANCING CRANE

Beloved Kuan Yin, Goddess calling through the Dancing Crane, may your sound, grace and light shine brighter than my doubt or fear. May your light help my own soul drawn near. May I surrender that which no longer serves me with unconditional love, and replace it with inspiration of your divine love. Om Shanti.

DANCE OF THE BUTTERFLY QUEEN

A pure heart and sincere love attracts divine grace. With the grace of Kuan Yin, Butterfly Queen, that which was impossible, becomes possible. From caterpillar to winged creature of delight, you cannot restrain what divine grace ordains no matter how incredible it may seem to be. Whatever has been troubling you, or whatever has been inspiring you, allow grace to infuse the situation or dream, so that it may unfold with divine perfection. Allow the Butterfly Queen to dance, she will bring healing and grace to your life situation now, beloved one, with lightness of step and grace in her heart.

*

PRAYER TO THE DANCING BUTTERFLY QUEEN

I now choose to surrender struggle and doubt and open to the blessings of Kuan Yin's divine grace, through which all manner of things become possible. Butterfly Queen, may I hear in my own heart the divine music of joy and peace to which you dance.
Om Mani Padme Hum.

DAUGHTER OF THE PHOENIX

When the soul is ready to spread its wings, it goes through a deep cleansing, purification and preparation for new levels of spiritual wisdom, power and light. Just like the Phoenix that is baptised through celestial fire to be born anew, you are going through such a phase of heavenly purification, preparation and initiation. This is an advanced phase of soul growth and soon after you will enjoy greater spiritual peace, divine power and advancement on your divine life path. Kuan Yin, Daughter of the Phoenix, has been through fire both physical and heavenly and has ascended into a position of great spiritual peace, power and authority. She guides you now to claim your rebirth and ascend.

*

A PRAYER TO THE DAUGHTER OF THE PHOENIX

Divine Daughter of the Phoenix, Mistress of Heavenly Fire, Kuan Yin, your light of peace and grace sustains me through the trials of my growth, may I be lifted by your luminous beauty into peace, may I feel rapture and excitement rather than fear and doubt as I grow. May I learn to release old pain without getting caught up in stories or history. May I have compassion for my own suffering as I release it with peace and love. May I live according to my truths, applying my own spiritual wisdom in all parts of my life with courage and faith. Om Mani Padme Hum.

DRINK FROM THE EMERALD FOUNTAIN

The Divine Feminine is encouraging of the awakening and empowerment of all living beings. When a sincere seeker is trying to find the way through, there is much help sent. It makes sense to be open to receive it, indeed to step forward and drink from the emerald fountain which is the unconditionally loving heart chakra of Kuan Yin. Allow yourself to be nourished by the power and love of the Divine Mother flowing to you now.

*

PRAYER AT THE EMERALD FOUNTAIN

Divine Kuan Yin, beloved Goddess that loves me unconditionally, you have my blessing and permission to assist me with divine energy that is for my highest good in all areas of my life now. I kneel at your sacred fountain of love, light and divine assistance now. I drink from your heart that which fills my soul! I gratefully receive your unconditionally loving help. Om Mani Padme Hum.

DYNASTY OF THE DIVINE MOTHER

The only wish of the Divine Mother Goddess is that all beings be spiritually free. The Divine Goddess calls us to realise our true nature, to fall in love with our own divinity. Enlightenment is a culmination of many small steps, each one as a drop of water forming a divine ocean of peace, realisation, love and unity within us, an ocean that washes away fear, separation and scarcity and bathes us in abundance and bliss. You carry the torch of enlightenment within you, beloved. Let it shine each day.

*

PRAYER TO THE DYNASTY OF THE DIVINE MOTHER

Beloved Kuan Yin, Green Tara, Mazu, Goddesses of the Great Divine Mother, please help me to live my light, to live my enlightenment in each day, to know my own self and to live the beauty and bliss with peace in my heart. Thank you for your help. Om Shanti. I feel your peace in my heart now. May all beings feel and know this peace within. Om Shanti. Om Mani Padme Hum.

EIGHT IMMORTALS

The messages you have been receiving that are unconditionally loving, fearless and encouraging of you to grow and be your true self are from your Higher Guidance. The Eight Immortals and other beings of divine light and divine love are guiding you. It is safe to follow these messages now. Doing so will bring you greater joy.

*

A PRAYER TO THE EIGHT IMMORTALS

I call upon the Eight Immortals that love me unconditionally and shine the light of peace and spiritual power upon me now, you understand that no matter what happens in life, there are blessings underneath it. Please help me find my clarity, wisdom, guidance and truths to reveal the blessings and grow now. Namaste, beloveds. Thank you for your help! Om Mani Padme Hum.

EMPRESS OF THE PEARL

You have an inner gift of great value, born of struggle, adversity and challenge. In wisdom you know that suffering can lead to growth provided we are willing to search for a way to heal through it. Seeing challenges as ways to expand your spiritual light empowers you to focus on the growing light, rather than getting caught up in suffering.

*

PRAYER TO THE EMPRESS OF THE PEARL

With beloved Kuan Yin, Empress of the Pearl, as my witness, I transform negativity into light through compassion. Anything that causes me discomfort I use to grow my light, so it becomes bigger than the discomfort, and I now choose to experience the light of my being and its spiritual growth as more powerful than any irritation or suffering which serves that growth.
Om Mani Padme Hum.

ENTER THE JADE TEMPLE

Kuan Yin, in her Temple of peaceful Jade, causes all conflict to elevate to higher peaceful resolution. A resolution and healing of any situation that is concerning you is already underway. In fact, you are being asked to begin to feel the relief of that resolution now, so you can more readily receive the divine solution and blessing of peace from the beloved Kuan Yin when it arrives.

*

PRAYER OF THE JADE TEMPLE

Om Shanti. Om Shanti. Om Mani Padme Hum.
Om Shanti. Om Shanti. May all beings know deep peace and blessings of beloved Priestess of Peace Kuan Yin. May the heart of all conflict be resolved in the Jade Temple. Om Shanti.
Om Shanti. Om Mani Padme Hum. Om Shanti. Om Shanti.

GATES OF HEAVEN

All beings have an ultimate spiritual destiny of happiness and
freedom. Beloved Kuan Yin shines tireless compassion upon all
life to this end. Yet sometimes attachments, lower vibrational
beings, entities and elementals become frightened of divine love
and believe they will do better to hide in human energy fields
instead. This blocks progress towards liberation where human
beings and lower vibrational beings can pass through the Gates
of Heaven into peace, bliss and homecoming to the spiritual
source of all life.

*

A PRAYER FOR RELEASE THROUGH
THE GATES OF HEAVEN

*May all beings be happy and free! May all beings be happy and
free! May all beings be happy and free! Lokah Sumastar Sukinoh
Bhavantu. Om Shanti, Shanti, Shanti. Om Mani Padme Hum.*

HEAR THE YELLOW TIGER MOTHER

Sometimes we must be strong and hold true whilst all around us seems to be shifting and changing. The Yellow Tiger Mother, Kuan Yin in her Guardian role, is roaring her divine sound within you. She asks you to hear her, to remember that you are a powerful being of light and even whilst you are in flow with universal forces, your strong roots help you be at peace with your truth, standing your ground whilst your light shines true.

*

PRAYER OF THE YELLOW TIGER MOTHER

Kuan Yin, beloved Yellow Tiger Mother, I need courage and strength now to be true to myself and allow my own light to take root and grow, nurture me with your strength of spirit so that I might realise that I have your strength within me too – it is my strength, my courageous heart. Help me, beloved, now, to realise my courage and have peace in my heart. I feel the roar of your courage and strength within me and I realise that this is my own courage too! Thank you for helping me realise this, beloved Tigress. Om Mani Padme Hum.

IMMORTAL TREASURES

You carry within you precious Immortal Treasures, beloved.
They exist beyond life and death, belonging to the celestial,
heavenly realms of the divine presence within you. Kuan Yin now
guides you to honour these treasures, the gifts of your soul, which
include the ability that you have to transmit healing. Honour
yourself as a healer, beloved. Whether formally or informally, your
soul brings a special healing light to humanity. You have divine
support in your role as a healer, in whatever way, usual or highly
unusual, that this is unfolding for you now.

*

PRAYER OF THE IMMORTAL TREASURES

Beloved Kuan Yin, may I feel the compassion that you have for me
within the depths of my own being. May I have compassion for myself
in the same way I do for others. May I accept and meet my needs
for wellness and fulfilment. May I receive healing with grace and
gratitude. I open now to fully receive, activate and shine forth the
Immortal Treasures in my own divine soul. Help me, beloved mother,
to do this with love, trust and grace. Om Mani Padme Hum.

IVORY SWAN GODDESS

The Ivory Swan Goddess speaks of spiritual grace and purity. The purity of your soul light never fades, beloved. Release guilt, shame, judgement or fear that you are not enough in any way, so that you may realise your beauty, be more of yourself and shine your divine essence into the world.

*

PRAYER OF THE IVORY SWAN GODDESS

Beloved Kuan Yin, Mother of Peace, Beauty and Compassion, the light in you is the same light in me! Help me to be at peace with my eternal innocence and purity. Ivory Swan Goddess, please help me let go of old beliefs and experiences of shame, self-condemnation or judgement that no longer serve me. I now honour and accept wholly and completely that the light in you is the same divine light in me. Om Mani Padme Hum.

MAIDEN MA GU

The Maiden Ma Gu, Goddess of Spring, healing and transformation, brings you assistance now. You are asked to honour that light can come from even the darkest beginnings, beloved one. In fact, sometimes we need to enter into the unknown parts of ourselves to find exactly what we need to grow in peace, creative self-fulfilment and happiness. The challenge can be to trust that we will arise from this darker place again. Just as the Spring always follows the Winter, beloved, so too will any inner work with the shadow precede a beautiful rebirth for you.

*

SPRING HEALING PRAYER OF KUAN YIN
AND MAIDEN MA GU

Beloved Kuan Yin and Spring Goddess Maiden Ma Gu, thank you for your unconditionally loving help now. I ask to be helped in knowing myself more fully and allowing that part of me that is seeking expression now, to emerge in a conscious, loving and empowering way. May I know and live all of myself, beloved ones, may my life be filled with light, energy and warmth, like Springtime after the Winter, for the highest good of all. Om Mani Padme Hum!

MANY HANDS OF THE GODDESS

The Goddess Kuan Yin brings blessings to multiple projects and many different parts of your life and consciousness, beloved. She is not limited to one task at a time. Do not be afraid to surrender into her guiding wisdom and creative genius now, for there is much that you can accomplish together and she wants to assist you!

*

A PRAYER TO THE MANY HANDS OF THE GODDESS

Hands that heal and bless, hands that lift and strengthen, hands that guide and hands that protect, Om Kuan Yin, Many Armed Mother of Mercy and Compassion, I receive your blessings and assistance now, for my highest good, so be it. Om Mani Padme Hum.

MOTHER FIERCE

Mother Fierce is your guardian. Nothing can penetrate the passionate fire of her fearless love. Your safety is assured, beloved. In the midst of any apparent challenge or threat, no matter how frightening it may seem, and no matter how insecure you might feel about taking a step on your spiritual path into more power, know that you are safe, you are protected, you are loved.

*

A PRAYER FOR THE FIERCE MOTHER

Take me into your heart, beloved Kuan Yin, fierce with love, where the pure fire of peace burns eternally, may I be blessed with peace and protection now and always, may I feel the loving protection of your consciousness within my own heart. Om Shanti, beloved. Om Mani Padme Hum.

MOTHER OF MERCY

Just like a sun that shines brightly casting a strong shadow, your growing spiritual power needs to be expressed with the awareness that it will have an effect on others, even if you are not completely conscious of that effect. To create peace in the expression of your power, we call upon the Mother of Mercy. Mercy tempers great strength and power with kindness, gentleness, compassion and caring. The Divine Kuan Yin brings the quality of mercy to you now as a divine gift, encouraging you to cultivate mercy in your dealings with others and to receive it for yourself now too.

*

PRAYER TO THE MOTHER OF MERCY

Mother of Mercy so loves my soul.
The Nectar of Mercy brings peace and bliss untold.
I open my heart now to this endless love and peace,
which the grace of Kuan Yin helps me reach.
Om Mani Padme Hum.

NECTAR OF THE LOTUS

The Divine Mother wishes that those who are meant to feed others be well fed too! Your devotion to helping others has the effect of squeezing the cosmic heart chakra of the Divine Mother. From her heart drips nectar, sweet, sustaining, life-affirming energy that feeds you and allows you to nourish many souls. Like a sacred chalice that overflows, when you are full, well and vital, the feeding of others happens effortlessly. You are guided to be fed now, fed with Divine Nectar from the Heart of the Mother.

*

PRAYER OF THE LOTUS NECTAR

Beloved Kuan Yin, help me realise the connection to myself and to life that I need to be able to live my highest vibrational life, where I am well, replenished, joyful and connected to the endless flow of divine energy and life force in our Universe. Please bring me clear guidance about how to best cultivate chi *now, how to be open to receive the Nectar of the Lotus, the life force and love of the Divine Mother, for my highest good, so be it. Om Mani Padme Hum.*

ORCHID PRIESTESS OF DESTINY

The Orchid Priestess of your highest spiritual destiny calls to you now, beloved. She calls you to your purpose, path and soul passion. You are called to rise again and again, to live up into your potential, with all its uniqueness and beauty. She will call you always, with her sweet flute playing deep in your heart, blossoms of orchid and chrysanthemum falling from her feet, stirring your heart to quest for your truest soul passion.

*

PRAYER TO THE ORCHID PRIESTESS OF DESTINY

My destiny is in my own heart, and you guide me deeper within myself, beloved Orchid Priestess, so I cannot miss out on anything that is divinely ordained for me! It will always find me! At peace in my heart, I now receive that which is guiding me in unconditional love into the fullness and expression of my own divine being. Om Mani Padme Hum.

PRINCESS OF THE AUTUMN HARVEST

The Princess of the Autumn Harvest brings gifts of bounty and blessing for efforts and actions of the past. It is a time when fruit of labours is ripe for the picking. A beautiful blessing is on its way to you now. This may come in the form of a spiritual gift, an opportunity, a windfall of abundance, a significant relationship or an important friendship and more. With gratitude in your heart, you will recognise the blessing when it comes to you and it will serve you perfectly. Be open to receive it, knowing it is justly deserved.

*

THE PRAYER OF DIVINE BLESSING
FROM THE PRINCESS OF THE AUTUMN HARVEST

I am divinely blessed, my heart is so full of blessing it overflows through my entire being and energy field. I receive blessings so easily. My joy inspires others to be open to blessings too. The Princess of the Autumn Harvest, Beloved Kuan Yin, knows my worthy heart and bestows abundant gifts to me now. Om Mani Padme Hum!

RADIANT MOON OF COMPASSION

Kuan Yin sits upon a Radiant Moon of Compassion, pouring forth the spiritual strength needed for you to liberate yourself from lower vibrational energies of fear and judgement, into the vibration of freedom, love and peace, where you naturally belong. You are being urged to use this power now to grow spiritually and free yourself from a situation that could draw you down.

*

PRAYER OF THE RADIANT MOON OF COMPASSION

Beloved Kuan Yin, your compassion empowers you with endless energy, patience, peace and love. Infuse me with your light and help me find my compassion so that I may rise above the energies of fear or judgement into greater compassion that liberates me to live my own life in peace. Shine upon me beloved Radiant Moon of Compassion. Om Kuan Yin. Om Mani Padme Hum.

REVEAL THE PEACOCK BEAUTY

The beauty of the peacock is breathtaking, with stunning lush colour unfolding in graceful and proud display. You too are a great beauty, beloved. Within you resides a glorious divine being of beautiful light, with an ability to create, as your divine birthright. The Peacock Beauty speaks to you of your creative energies rising to sublime, inspired new levels as you are accessing the power of your throat chakra for higher creation. Your intentions, decisions and particularly your words, are becoming more powerful.

Enjoy the wise use of this growing creative potency to express the beauty within you, asking for divine blessing on all your plans, projects and words.

*

PRAYER TO THE PEACOCK BEAUTY

Beloved Kuan Yin, bless me with the grace to surrender into the beauty of my own soul, to recognise my higher creativity in flow now, to make the creations of my soul my highest priority, that I may live with abundance, peace and happiness. Help me, beloved beauty, to recognise my own beauty, as magnificent and colourful as the stunning peacock. May my creations be as lovely. Om Mani Padme Hum.

SACRED RIVER YANGTZE

The Sacred River Yangtze eternally flows and changes. Just as
the river flows and changes course, you too are evolving in your
divine path. Veils and sheaths that once covered your soul light
are being washed away. Cleansing by sacred water specifically
indicates that your emotional life and your life direction are being
purified and healed. Changes in the flow of energy within you
and in the momentum of your life path unfolding are imminent.
This is exciting! You are growing and changing and soon your life
circumstances will reflect your inner evolution.

*

PRAYER AT THE SACRED RIVER YANGTZE

*Kuan Yin, Divine Ancient River Mother, Sacred Soul of the Yangtze,
I receive the spiritual waters of your cleansing and illumination
now. Bless my path and my process with your mercy and potency.
May I reveal and realise myself in a new way now, without fear or
attachment to the past, may I allow the Sacred River to chart my
course, carving out my highest divine destiny and path now, of my
own free will, so be it. Om Mani Padme Hum.*

SHINING LOTUS

There are times when it makes sense to be discrete, until you find your inner strength so that you feel empowered enough to share your thoughts, feelings and beliefs without wavering, even in the face of challenge by another. At other times, we benefit ourselves and others by taking a risk and allowing the inner lotus blossom of our true self to shine forth, for all to behold.

*

PRAYER OF THE SHINING LOTUS

Beloved Kuan Yin, mother of mercy and compassion, bless me with divine timing and divine words, that I may express myself truthfully and well, and that my truths may be healing for all concerned, for the highest good, so be it! Bless my lotus heart, with shining peace and love. Om Mani Padme Hum.

SISTERS OF THE STAR BLOSSOMS

It is good to remember that whilst we each take our own unique journey back into divine bliss and truth, we have plenty of friends that love us unconditionally and wish to help us find the way home with the least suffering and greatest joy. When we allow ourselves to be helped, we help others too. It is a spiral of support and love that is wishing to connect more so with you now.

*

PRAYER TO THE SISTERS OF THE STAR BLOSSOMS

I call upon the unconditional love of the Sisters of the Star Blossoms and of Beloved Kuan Yin, please help me know when to step back and when to step forward into group energy. Help me rise above my fears of being lost or consumed or hurt, and help me not hide in a group either. Help me know my own light and be able to share it fearlessly and with mercy and compassion with others. Help me find my rightful place within group energy now, beloveds, for the greatest good, so be it! Om Shanti.

SISTERS OF THE SUN RISING

You are a highly creative being with the potential to help raise the vibration of consciousness on this planet through your creative projects, work, dreams and hobbies. The power of collaboration, choosing to work with others in joint projects, allows for synergy to occur where you can grow stronger and become more than the sum of your individual parts, calling in great cosmic assistance and potency! You are guided to remain open to other souls joining forces with you. Just like the Sisters of the Sun Rising that bring great energy to help humanity through their group endeavours, when you allow for aligned group effort, much that is wonderful can occur.

*

A PRAYER OF THE SISTERS OF THE SUN RISING

Beloved Sisters of the Sun Rising, sweet sister Kuan Yin, thank you for your help now in opening my heart fearlessly with confidence, faith, friendliness, firm boundaries and an open mind to be inspired, supported and helped in making successful creative collaborations. May all such relationships be blessed in my life now. Om Mani Padme Hum.

SOUND THE FIERCE FLUTE

Discernment empowers you to make choices that are aligned with your spiritual intentions. Like a fierce sounding flute cutting through all vibrations with purity and intent, your discernment allows you to stay true to your values and spiritual destiny, without getting caught up in distraction. If you wish to grow spiritually through love, joy, peace and abundance, then discerning between higher and lower vibrational choices is helpful.

*

A PRAYER FOR THE FIERCE FLUTE

Dearest Kuan Yin, who sees from the highest perspective and knows the truths in all situations, please help me discern the best possible choices available to me. Bless me with the awareness I need to make choices that support my deepest desires this lifetime. May my spiritual intentions be blessed and manifest. Help me see beyond illusion, beloved, into the deeper truth of matters. Sound your flute so fierce with love and compassion and clarity now. Om Mani Padme Hum.

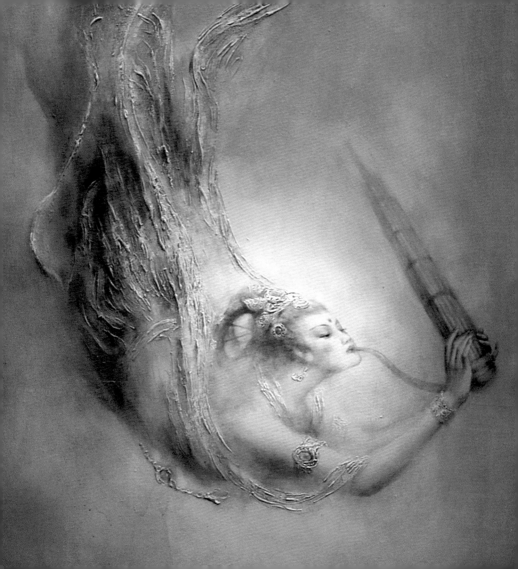

SPIN THE SILKEN THREAD DIVINE

In creating precious silks there is a sorting process, sifting out that which is broken to find that which is precious and pure. You are commencing a new cycle, beloved, and it is time to allow for that which is more precious and pure, that which you wish to take with you into the future, to continue and to release that which does not align with your true heart. Sometimes we need to help ourselves access the new cycle by releasing vows from this or other lifetimes, releasing old emotional patterns and calling in wisdom and talents from past lifetimes. You are guided to accept this healing now.

*

PRAYER TO SPIN THE SILKEN THREAD DIVINE

I now choose to release all vows, agreements, veils and cords that are not based in unconditional love and no longer serve my highest good, through the divine mercy, compassion and power of Kuan Yin, and my own free will, I let this go. I now call upon my past life and current life mastery, according to my own free will and through the unconditional love and divine mercy of Kuan Yin, this is so. I choose to spin the silken thread divine, my own soul light, into my life now. Om Mani Padme Hum!

SWEEPING SISTER WILLOW

Sweeping Sister Willow gently brings you healing for forgiveness and release of old pain now. Let her branches gracefully sweep any sadness and pain from your heart and soul. Your time for greater inner freedom is dawning and the cleansing sadness and healing of forgiveness is the pathway to that greater freedom now. You deserve this freedom and you are swiftly becoming ready to gift it to yourself with the help of Kuan Yin.

*

PRAYER OF SWEEPING SISTER WILLOW

Beloved Kuan Yin, Sweeping Sister Willow, with gracefulness and surrender into love, you forgave great transgressions against you because you chose wisdom and spiritual growth. You did not hide your anger, you simply chose to let it go and find peace and compassion in your heart. You were free to ascend into bliss! Please bless me that I may draw upon my own wisdom and spiritual strength to forgive and empower myself now. I allow Sweeping Sister Willow to gently wash my heart clean.
Om Mani Padme Hum.

TAI CHI RISING

Your energy field is growing stronger, with more spiritual electricity pulsing through your being. Take time to nourish your nervous system as it adjusts and be gentle with yourself as you adjust to increasing levels of spiritual potency, which gives more impact to your words, actions and thoughts.

*

A PRAYER FOR TAI CHI RISING

Through the mercy and compassion of Kuan Yin, and my own free will, may my energy field grow to meet the needs of my soul light. May I be strong and merciful, powerful and wise in equal measure, may I be loving and potent with temperance and peaceful intention. Om Mani Padme Hum.

TEN SISTERS OF LIGHT

You are an advanced soul and have lived many incarnations, shone your light through many different faces. Your soul has learned many skills in past lives, developed abilities and talents. This lifetime is a culminating lifetime in the sense that your soul is drawing together potencies developed over many lifetimes into unified expression. It is like drawing on the power of ten sisters, or more, into your one current lifetime. Be prepared to grow and shine, beloved.

*

PRAYER TO THE TEN SISTERS OF LIGHT

Divine Kuan Yin, Om Namaha, I call upon the Ten Sisters of Light that love me unconditionally, I call upon your grace, protection and assistance now in releasing past life wounds and patterns so that more of my soul light can manifest in present time. Please bless this process with your mercy, compassion and grace. Thank you, beloveds. Om Mani Padme Hum.

THE AMARYLLIS LUTE

You have won a victory beloved, a victory over the past and the Amaryllis Lute is sounding through every cell of your being, heralding your rising vibration as you leave fear behind you once again. In fact the Lute says you are growing fast and spiritually, you are outgrowing your old life even more so. When your vibration changes, so too does your life, beloved. This is natural. It is safe and loving for you to release that which no longer feels right for you, no matter how much it was important in your old life, it might not have the same place in your new life.

*

PRAYER TO THE AMARYLLIS LUTE

Your beauty triumphs, your sound so pure causes my heart to soar.
My vibration rises and my cells are flooded with divine light.
I know myself as Love. Om Mani Padme Hum!

THE BOOK OF CHANGES

Just like a beautiful but unusual melody, the divine plan is unfolding through your life, although it isn't always predictable! Kuan Yin is guiding you in the right direction. Even if you do not fully understand what is happening in your life right now, allow Kuan Yin to bless you with trust in the unfoldment of your own divine path. The Book of Changes is always at play, helping us find our way. You are just taking a smarter route to your destination!

*

A PRAYER TO HONOUR THE BOOK OF CHANGES

Beloved Kuan Yin, thank you for your blessings of divine grace and assistance through my life as I allow the divine plan, the Book of Changes with all its wisdom, to simply flow with trust and faith. I now pray for the courage to trust in your goodness and assistance, to see the beauty and perfection of all life situations so that I may benefit from it greatly now. Thank you for your help. Om Shanti. May I feel your peace in my heart now. Om Shanti.

THE DANCE UNVEILING

There is a situation in your life that is about to reveal itself to you with greater clarity. Just like sands shifting, the picture will seem clearer and quite different to how it once appeared to you. This clarity will bring you great relief and confirmation of your intuition. Be patient and allow the revelation to come to you at the perfect time.

*

A PRAYER FOR THE DANCE UNVEILING

Beloved Kuan Yin, I now let go of any fear that would distort my perception and prevent me from beholding the highest levels of truth which I am capable of perceiving. Help me now, beloved one, with your divine dance of mercy and compassion, that the confusion may clear, any distortion may be released, and the truth be revealed with grace and simplicity. Unveil the truths with your dance of grace, beloved. Thank you. Om Mani Padme Hum.

THE LOTUS THRONE

The same Lotus wisdom that enlightens beloved Kuan Yin and all spiritual masters is the very same Lotus Light within your own heart, beloved. It can take great courage to trust your own inner light, to ascend the throne of your own inner spiritual authority, especially if the light of others around you seems more powerful than your own. You are being asked to trust this inner guidance above all others now. Have faith in your own heart. Know that you are divine.

*

PRAYER OF THE LOTUS THRONE

You burn bright in my heart, guiding me eternally, Divine Lotus of Light, my very own heart. I ascend to the Lotus Throne within you, my power, my wisdom, my love and light acknowledged. All is well within my own soul, by Kuan Yin's grace and my own divine fire. I trust and empower myself spiritually now more than ever. Om Mani Padme Hum.

THE TAO

The Tao is always flowing, always nourishing life into creation, always presenting steps and solutions and always reminding us that we are perfection in this moment. You are being guided to relax and allow life to flow.

*

PRAYER TO THE TAO

Guide me. Restore me. I trust you completely. Your wisdom, love and joy lights my path and the way becomes easy for me.
Om Mani Padme Hum.

THE THRESHOLD

At the Threshold you stand. Before you lies a way of being that is beyond fear. It is a sacred passing through a karmic veil into a new life of empowerment, peace, spiritual service to humanity and joy in your own soul.

✶

PRAYER FOR THE PASSING OF THE THRESHOLD

May I be blessed under the compassionate love and protection of Kuan Yin as my soul prepares to cross the threshold from fear to love in all dimensions of my being. Om Mani Padme Hum, Om Mani Padme Hum, Om Mani Padme Hum.

THE YIN EMPRESS

The Yin Empress brings peace, prosperity and success to her beloved devotees. Your soul purpose includes healing and empowerment of the Divine Feminine, the Yin Empress herself. You gain power, assistance and untold blessings in following your soul purpose. You are lifted and supported in your sacred work now.

*

PRAYER TO THE YIN EMPRESS

Divine Yin Empress, Mother of Compassion, Kuan Yin, Om Namaha. Peace, grace, light and feminine power infuse your being within my heart now. May I be a vessel of the grace and healing of the divine feminine. May I live my soul truths on this planet, may fear and anger be softened with love, may I find the true nature of my spiritual power and may I align with you, beloved, into eternal Grace of Divine Love. My devotion to the Yin Empress and her wish for all beings to be spiritually free grows in my heart now, I receive your love and protection. Om Mani Padme Hum.

TO THE CELESTIAL MOUNTAIN

There are times when divine energy is needed to help us achieve our spiritual goals. When you do not feel completely in control of your destiny, the divine is usually gifting you with an opportunity to reach for assistance and to invoke divine power, to call to the celestial mountain so that you might be gifted with a far superior outcome. Your permission to beings that love you unconditionally to offer you help is an expression of spiritual empowerment, you empower those forces to come to your aid and help you manifest your life purpose and destiny.

*

A PRAYER TO THE CELESTIAL MOUNTAIN

Beloved Kuan Yin, in the Ashram of your Celestial Mountain, hear me, please help me to let go of my difficulties in receiving help, in any feelings of worthlessness or distrust that prevent me from being guided, moved and placed in positions of divine assistance for my greatest good. Help me feel worthy of help and help me receive that help which comes to me in unconditional love now. Thank you! Om Mani Padme Hum.

TURQUOISE LOTUS MOTHER

Turquoise Lotus Mother brings precious healing to you now.
Allow yourself to be lifted out of your struggle, beloved one.
An old pattern is finally in its death throes, something that
weighed heavily on you from your past. This can be one of the
most testing times to allow something to go, just when it seems
to be so demanding of your time, focus and attention. Yet do not
doubt, you have actually learned the lessons it required of you
and now you are being blessed with an opportunity to receive
karmic healing.

*

PRAYER TO THE TURQUOISE LOTUS MOTHER

*Beloved Kuan Yin, Turquoise Lotus Mother, I now let go of any
unhelpful pride or restrictive beliefs that would stop me from
receiving the divine grace of karmic healing through you now.
I ask that my soul be blessed, and that I receive the full bestowal of
grace to which I am spiritually entitled, with gratitude and love,
I open my heart to you now. Om Mani Padme Hum.*

VALE OF SHADOWS

A lotus blossoms with deep rich mud into which she plunges her roots and draws great nourishment. From this mud, made of water and earth, growth happens and great beauty is revealed. Your soul lotus thrives through depth of emotion and aliveness of your body into which she can plant her self and unfold as a lotus of light.

*

A PRAYER FOR ASSISTANCE THROUGH THE VALE OF SHADOWS

I pray to Kuan Yin, beloved spiritual mother, please help me be fearless in the Vale of Shadows, realising that I am just growing in self-awareness. May whatever has grown ugly through lack of love gleam like a polished jewel through my attention, willingness to love and accept all parts of me and my divinely-inspired creativity in integrating this part of me into my life with more consciousness. Om Mani Padme Hum. May all parts of me be blessed. Om Mani Padme Hum.

WEAVE THE FUTURE GOLDEN

Something good is coming your way! Kuan Yin urges you to weave your future into the present moment, to call in and draw to you the opportunities, teachings, circumstances and synchronicities waiting for you, that will enable your soul to live its divine destiny with greater abundance, bliss and creative fulfilment.

*

A PRAYER TO WEAVE THE GOLDEN FUTURE

Beloved Kuan Yin, thank you for being my spiritual witness – beyond time and space there is only love, truth, bliss and joy – and I now choose to dip into the waters of my own divine essence to call into the present moment the good that has vested for me spiritually. I ask for the grace, wisdom and skill needed to put this future good into perfect expression in the present moment. May I weave my future golden into this present moment. Thank you!
Om Mani Padme Hum.

About the Author

Alana Fairchild is a Soul Whisperer devoted to the awakening of your soul so that you may live your highest divine destiny this lifetime. Alana lives and breathes the Divine and invites you to do the same through her music, voice, meditations, and writings, all offered in service to your own divine awakening and inspiration.

Alana is the creator of numerous meditation CDs by Blue Angel including *Inner Power, Star Child, Ganesha, Past Life Healing, Isis: Power of the Priestess, Divine Lotus Mother: Meditations with Kuan Yin, Radiance* and *Mystical Healing*.

Visit Alana at **www.alanafairchild.com** where you can find Alana's full product range by Blue Angel including the best-selling oracle decks *Kuan Yin Oracle, Mother Mary Oracle* and *Isis Oracle* and her books *Crystal Angels 444* and *Crystal Masters 333*.

About the Artist

Zeng Hao is a gifted young painter with a deep love for ancient Chinese culture. He uses mainly classical western oil painting techniques to create his large works of art. Born in the city Zigong of Sichuan province, Zeng Hao first developed an interest in painting under the influence of his artist father and later attended the Sichuan Art College. When Zeng Hao first visited Dunhuang, an ancient and once important city whose name means 'brilliant and magnificent', to observe and study Dunhuang art, he was amazed and inspired by the beauty and splendour of the art in the Mogao Cave. Dunhuang is along the Silk Road which once linked the East and West, and through his love of Dunhuang Art, Zeng Hao has fused classic western and eastern ideals of beauty in the images and Goddesses he creates. Zeng Hao talks about a tranquil, peaceful and romantic paradise that exists deep in his heart and feels the Dunhuang Goddess is a real goddess that exists inside his heart – she is the embodiment of pure truth, goodness and beauty. Zeng Hao is a member of the Dunhuang Creative Centre of Arts Association and his work is receiving great acclaim both in China and internationally.

You can see more of Zeng Hao's work by visiting his website:
www.zhdhart.com

For more information on this
or any Blue Angel Publishing release,
please visit our website at:

www.blueangelonline.com